HIP-HOP & R&B

Culture, Music & Storytelling

Chance the Rapper

HIP-HOP & R&B

Culture, Music & Storytelling

Beyoncé

Bruno Mars

Cardi B

Chance the Rapper

DJ Khaled

Drake

Jay-Z

Pharrell

Pitbull

Rihanna

The Weeknd

MC

MASON CREST

Joe L. Morgan

HIP-HOP & R&B

Chance the Rapper

Culture, Music & Storytelling

Mason Crest
450 Parkway Drive, Suite D
Broomall, Pennsylvania 19008
(866) MCP-BOOK (toll free)

First printing
9 8 7 6 5 4 3 2 1

hardback: 978-1-4222-4179-0
series: 978-1-4222-4176-9
ebook: 978-1-4222-7621-1

Library of Congress Cataloging-in-Publication Data

Names: Morgan, Joe L. author.
Title: Chance the Rapper / Joe L. Morgan.
Description: Broomall, PA : Mason Crest, 2018. | Series: Hip-hop & R&B: culture, music & storytelling.
Identifiers: LCCN 2018020769 (print) | LCCN 2018021052 (ebook) | ISBN 9781422276211 (eBook) | ISBN 9781422241790 (hardback) | ISBN 9781422241769 (series)
Subjects: LCSH: Chance the Rapper--Juvenile literature. | Rap musicians--United States--Biography--Juvenile literature.
Classification: LCC ML3930.C442 (ebook) | LCC ML3930.C442 M67 2018 (print) | DDC 782.421649092 [B] --dc23
LC record available at https://lccn.loc.gov/2018020769

Developed and Produced by National Highlights, Inc.
Editor: Susan Uttendorfsky
Interior and cover design: Annalisa Gumbrecht, Studio Gumbrecht
Production: Michelle Luke

NATIONAL
HIGHLIGHTS

QR CODES AND LINKS TO THIRD-PARTY CONTENT

CONTENTS

KEY ICONS TO LOOK FOR:

Words to understand: These words with their easy-to-understand definitions will increase the reader's understanding of the text while building vocabulary skills.

Sidebars: This boxed material within the main text allows readers to build knowledge, gain insights, explore possibilities, and broaden their perspectives by weaving together additional information to provide realistic and holistic perspectives.

Educational videos: Readers can view videos by scanning our QR codes, providing them with additional educational content to supplement the text. Examples include news coverage, moments in history, speeches, iconic sports moments, and much more!

Text-dependent questions: These questions send the reader back to the text for more careful attention to the evidence presented there.

Research projects: Readers are pointed toward areas of further inquiry connected to each chapter. Suggestions are provided for projects that encourage deeper research and analysis.

Series of glossary of key terms: This back-of-the-book glossary contains terminology used throughout this series. Words found here increase the reader's ability to read and comprehend higher-level books and articles in this field.

Chapter 1:

Chance the Rapper's Highlights Reel

Chance the Rapper has produced thirty-four mixtapes that are available by digital download. A total of five singles have reached the *Billboard* Top 100 Chart, including one that secured the number one overall spot. Overall, his music has been downloaded or shared several million times. With a tremendously successful career so far—by the young age of twenty-four—Chance the Rapper has had a definite effect on the music industry and the accessibility of music.

This rising star in the world of hip-hop puts out music that is a mix of uplifting beats, jazz influence, and lyrics about his struggles with his Christian roots. Highlighted throughout this chapter are noteworthy moments, singles, and top mixtape downloads that have shaped his hip-hop career into what it is today.

Chance the Rapper's Playlist

10 Day
(Released April 03, 2012)

The singer's debut mixtape was released independently in 2012 through DatPiff.com, a platform that bills itself as "The Authority in Free Mixtapes." The recording, which received critical acclaim, was written in response to a ten-day suspension he received while attending William Jones College Preparatory High School in downtown Chicago. Of particular importance is the single *Windows*, which he released in December 2011. This song served as Chance the Rapper's announcement to the world of hip-hop that he was moving onto the scene.

Collaborations

- *Windows*, featuring Alex Wiley and Akenya
- *Family*, featuring Vic Mensa and Sulaiman
- *Long Time II*, featuring Donnie Trumpet
- *Hey Ma*, featuring Lili K and Peter Cottontale

ACID RAP
(Released April 30, 2013)

The second release from Chance the Rapper received wide critical acclaim. After touring with Donald Glover (aka Childish Gambino), Chance the Rapper released his second production on April 30, 2013, through the digital download service DatPiff.com. The thirteen-song sophomore offering has been his most successful effort to date, with downloads totaling nearly 1.6 million. It has also been shared among users more than 2.7 million times. The release features collaborations with Twista, Vic Mensa, Noname Gypsy, and other big stars of hip-hop.

Collaborations

- *Good Ass Intro*, featuring BJ the Chicago Kid, Lili K, Kiara, Will of the O'My's, J.P. Floyd, and Peter Cottontale

Scan the code here to listen to listen to *Favorite Song*, one of the several big-name collaborative singles from Chance the Rapper's second recording, Acid Rap

- *Pusha Man*, featuring Lili K and Nate Fox

- *Cocoa Butter Kisses*, featuring Vic Mensa and Twista

- *Lost*, featuring Noname Gypsy

- *Everybody's Something*, featuring BJ the Chicago Kid and Saba

- *Favorite Song*, featuring Donald Glover as Childish Gambino

- *NaNa*, featuring Action Bronson

- *Smoke Again*, featuring Ab-Soul

Good Enough
(Released December 11, 2013)

This mixtape was discovered on a forgotten Facebook page and released to the internet via Reddit. According to a user named "Lavmar," who spoke in an interview with MTV,

> *I found Chance the Rapper's old Facebook [account] yesterday and got a bunch of old pics/vids/music. Here's 2 of his earlier mixtapes. [The release also included the mixtape* Back To School Pack.*] Enjoy, I'm a huge Chance fan and it's cool as hell hearing his real old s--t like this so I thought y'all would like to hear it too. There's actually some good s--t on those mixtapes.*

There were no collaborations noted in this release, but Good Enough, with nine songs—including one of the same title—further defined Chance the Rapper's style and highlighted the ease with which a mix of musical influences were shaping his successful career. The production has been downloaded nearly 100,000 times via DatPiff.com, with over 100,000 audio plays through the website.

Scan the code here to listen to listen to the song *Good Enough*

Back to School Pack EP
(Released December 11, 2013)

As mentioned, this extended-play mixtape was also released through Reddit by user

"Lavmar" along with Good Enough on December 11, 2013. The recording included collaborations of five songs, which are:

- *In the Pen Dance*, featuring Nico Segal
- *Nostalgia*
- *Dear Chicago Summer*
- *Kick Back*, featuring Joey Davis and Zekur
- *September 7th*, featuring Akenya and Nico Segal

The song *September 7th* has neo-soul influences reminiscent of Erykah Badu, Jill Scott, and Ledisi, as well as a mix of Sarah Vaughan scat and cool jazz trumpet. The Back to School Pack EP has been downloaded, so far, more than 87,000 times from DatPiff.com, and listened to nearly 95,000 times.

Free EP

(Released August 05, 2015)

The production Free was released in collaboration with solo hip-hop artist Lil B on August 05, 2015. This freestyle-based mixtape was made up of free-flowing raps and tunes. So far, it has been downloaded nearly 68,000 times on DatPiff.com and listened to 169,000 times.

Scan the code here to listen to the song *September 7th*, one of the singles off the mixtape Back to School Pack EP

Scan the code here to listen to the single *Last Dance* from the mixtape FREE

Collaborations, all featuring Lil B

- *Last Dance*
- *What's Next*
- *First Mixtape*
- *Amen*
- *Do My Dance*
- *We Rare*

COLORING BOOK

(Released May 13, 2016)

This recording was released exclusively through Apple Music on May 13, 2016, and via other services—such as DatPiff.com and SoundCloud—on May 27, 2016. The mixtape received overwhelming positive reviews for Chance the Rapper, and its success established him as one of hip-hop's newest ambassadors and stars. The mixtape features a who's who lineup of hip-hop and pop stars, including collaborations with Kanye West, Lil Wayne, 2 Chainz, Young Thug, Saba, Future, and Justin Bieber.

COLORING BOOK is Chance the Rapper's second most popular mixtape release, behind his sophomore release ACID RAP. The recording has been downloaded more than half a million times and listened to over 2.2 million times, according to music listing service DatPiff.com.

Collaborations

- *All We Got*, featuring Kanye West and the Chicago Children's Choir
- *No Problem*, featuring Lil Wayne and 2 Chainz
- *Summer Friends*, featuring Jeremih and Francis and the Lights
- *Mixtape*, featuring Lil Yachty and Young Thug
- *Angels*, featuring Saba
- *Juke Jam*, featuring Justin Bieber and Towkio
- *All Night*, featuring Knox Fortune
- *How Great*, featuring Jay Electronica and My Cousin Nicole
- *Smoke Break*, featuring Future
- *Finish Line/Drown*, featuring T-Pain, Kirk Franklin, Noname, and Eryn Allen Kane

T-Pain, Supafest 2012, Sydney, Australia — Eva Rinaldi photographer

Scan the code here to listen to the Grammy Award–winning single *No Problem* from Chance the Rapper's critically acclaimed mixtape COLORING BOOK

MERRY CHRISTMAS LIL' MAMA
(Released December 22, 2016)

MERRY CHRISTMAS LIL' MAMA was a collaborative release of nine songs with hip-hop artist Jeremih. The recording featured the soulful title track *Merry Christmas Lil' Mama*, along with several collaborations. These collaborations featured artists King Louie (who appeared on the first track *All the Way* and the title song), Lud Foe, and Noname Gypsy.

All the Way also included a performance by comedian and Bill Cosby–critic Hannibal Buress, a sometime-star of the Comedy Central hit series *Broad Street*, which features Ilana Glazer and Abbi Jacobson. DatPiff.com stats say the song has over 100,000 downloads to its credit and more than 308,900 audio plays.

Collaborations

- *All the Way*, featuring Hannibal Buress and King Louie
- *I Shoulda Left You*, featuring Lud Foe
- *The Tragedy*, featuring Noname Gypsy
- *Merry Christmas Lil' Mama*, featuring King Louie

CHANCE THE RAPPER x VIC MENSA

(Released March 08, 2014)

This self-titled production included a collaboration with hip-hop star Vic Mensa, along with involvement from several of hip-hop's biggest stars. The eleven-song mixtape brought with it the talents of Twista, Lil Wayne, Kids These Days, Sulaiman, Disclosure, and Alex Wiley. The stats for the recording from DatPiff.com show that as of November 2017, it has been downloaded more than 11,000 times and listened to more than 34,000.

Collaborations

- *Cocoa Butter Kisses*, featuring Twista
- *Wasting Time*, featuring Kids These Days
- *Family*, featuring Sulaiman
- *When a Fire Starts to Burn,* featuring Vic Mensa and Disclosure
- *You Song*, featuring Lil Wayne
- *Feel That*, featuring Vic Mensa
- *Naked Pictures*, featuring Vic Mensa
- *Spaceship II*, featuring Alex Wiley and GLC

Scan the code here to listen to the title single *Merry Christmas Lil' Mama* from Chance the Rapper's December 2016 mixtape of the same name

CHANCE

(Released May 08, 2014)

After the release of CHANCE THE RAPPER x VIC MENSA, the artist followed up with a solo project simply titled CHANCE in 2014. The mixtape, which has been downloaded more than 10,000 times and listened to over 26,500 times, contains seventeen tracks. The usual cast of characters that Chance the Rapper has grown to respect and work with in the industry participated in this production: Calliko, Sir Michael Rocks, Vic Mensa, Ab-Soul, Saba, and Twista.

Two of the singles, *The Worst Guys* and *Favorite Song*, feature hip-hop artist Childish Gambino.

Vic Mensa

Those familiar with television sitcoms know him as actor Donald Glover from the NBC show *Community*. Glover's success on *Community* as a comedian—and also as a former writer for NBC's *Saturday Night Live*—allowed him to appeal to a wider audience as creator, director, and star of the FX Network's show *Atlanta*. Glover became the first African-American in 2017 to win a prime-time director's Emmy Award for his work on *Atlanta*.

Collaborations

- *The Worst Guys*, featuring Childish Gambino (aka Donald Glover)
- *1985*, featuring Calliko
- *Too Late*, featuring Sir Michael Rocks
- *Tweakin'*, featuring Vic Mensa
- *Smoke Again*, featuring Ab-Soul
- *Come Up*, featuring Calliko
- *Everybody's Something*, featuring Saba and BJ the Chicago Kid
- *Cocoa Butter Kisses,* featuring Vic Mensa and Twista
- *Favorite Song*, featuring Childish Gambino
- *Suitcase*, featuring Vic Mensa
- *High Life*, featuring Calliko

Twista

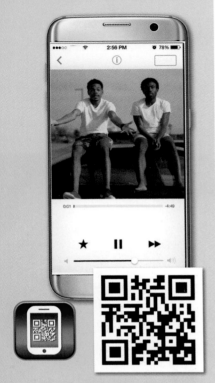

Scan the code to listen to *The Worst Guys* from Chance, which includes hip-hop artist and rapper Childish Gambino—also known to television fans as Donald Glover from the *NBC* series *Community* and the award-winning FX Network series *Atlanta*

Acid Rap 2
(Released June 18, 2014)

Acid Rap, released in 2013, served notice to the world of hip-hop that a new star had arrived. The thirteen-song mixtape—with its mix of jazz, soul, gospel, and rhythm and blues (R&B)—put Chance the Rapper front and center among the biggest stars in this kind of music and established him as one to watch in the future.

The 2014 release of Acid Rap 2, a sequel of sorts, brought in one familiar rapping partner, Twista, as well as some new collaborators. The downloadable version of the recording, available on DatPiff.com, features three bonus tracks, two of which were from live performances (*Paradise* and *Wonderful Day*). The effort was received with fair success, so far being downloaded 26,000 times on DatPiff.com, with over 39,000 audio plays.

Collaborations

- *Home Studio (Back in This B##@)*, featuring The Social Experiment (SoX)

- *Such a Thing*, featuring B-Legit

- *I Am Very Very Lonely*, featuring SoX

- *Steamer*, featuring Brian Fresco, Vic Mensa, Kami de Chukwu, and Tokyo Shawn

- *Ridin' Round*, featuring Ego
- *Bout a Dolla*, featuring The O'My's, Chip tha Ripper, Chuck Inglish, and Twista

Chance the Rapper on Tour

As referenced earlier, Childish Gambino asked Chance the Rapper to join his first concert tour of North America as his opening act. Childish Gambino's 2012 Camp Tour began on April 02, 2012, at the University of Iowa's main lounge in Iowa City and was scheduled to run until August 10, with a final show at the Hollywood Palladium in Los Angeles, California.

From there, Chance the Rapper went on to star in his own Social Experiment Tour, which began in Champaign, Illinois, on October 25. The last show was on December 19, 2013.

Additionally, he participated in the Verge Campus Tour (in which he was featured) that took place in the fall of 2014. The tour also featured the artists Sweater Beats and Young & Sick.

The Magnificent Coloring World Tour was Chance the Rapper's next performing excursion. It

Rapper Childish Gambino performs on stage at the iHeartRadio Music Festival

began in San Diego, California, on September 15, 2016. He announced the tour through an event called the Magnificent Coloring Day Festival, which was held at U.S. Cellular Field in Chicago on September 24, 2016. The jaunt featured such acts as Francis and the Lights, Skrillex, John Legend, the comedian Hannibal Buress, Alicia Keys, 2 Chainz, Common, and Kanye West.

Award-Winning Collaborations

Acid Rap

(Released April 30, 2013)

This mixtape includes Chance the Rapper's first widely acclaimed collaborations. The production received a Best Mixtape nomination at the 2013 BET Hip-Hop Awards. Twista, Vic Mensa, Noname Gypsy, and others collaborated with Chance the Rapper on the recording.

Coloring Book

(Released May 13, 2016)

This Chance the Rapper release was far and away his most successful. The mixtape was honored as Best Rap Album at the 2017 Grammy Awards (which also garnered a Best Rap Performance Grammy for the single *No Problem* and Best New Artist award for Chance the Rapper).

The mixtape also received the 2017 BET Hip-Hop Award for Best Mixtape, alongside his main collaborators Lil Wayne and 2 Chainz. Other collaborators on the production include Kanye West and Young Thug.

In line with the great reviews this mixtape received, it was nominated for multiple awards:

- BET Hip-Hop Award Lyricist of the Year for 2016 and 2017
- BET Hip-Hop Award Hot Ticket Performer for 2016
- BET Hip-Hop Award MVP of the Year for 2017
- BET Hip-Hop Award Hustler of the Year for 2017
- BET Award Album of the Year for 2017
- NAACP Image Awards Outstanding Album for 2017
- NAACP Image Awards Outstanding Male Artist for 2017
- NME Award Best International Male Artist for 2017
- Shorty Award Best in Music for 2017
- Soul Train Music Awards, Best Gospel/ Inspirational Award Best in Music for 2017

No Problem
(Released May 26, 2016)

Written by Chance the Rapper and Lil Wayne, and sung with 2 Chainz, this single from the COLORING BOOK mixtape received the 2017 Grammy Award for Best Rap Performance.

Continuing the song's success, it also received the 2017 BET Award for Best Collaboration and was nominated for multiple other awards.

- Grammy Award Best Rap Song for 2017
- BET Award Best Male Hip-Hop Artist for 2017
- Soul Train Music Awards, Rhythm & Bars Award Best New Artist for 2017
- Soul Train Music Award for 2017
- Teen Choice Award Choice R&B/Hip-Hop Artist for 2017

Collaborating and Performing with Other Artists

The young artist made an impression on fans with his performance at the 2015 Bonnaroo Music Festival held in Manchester, Tennessee, as part of the Superjam concert collection. He additionally performed alongside rapper Kendrick Lamar and the legendary group Earth, Wind & Fire, who were among the Class of 2000's Rock and Roll Hall of Fame inductees.

Hip-hop recording artist Tauheed Epps, aka 2 Chainz, attends the Top Five premiere at the Ziegfeld Theatre

Chance the Rapper became a key part of Kanye West's 2016 album, THE LIFE OF PABLO. He co-wrote and performed on several of the album's tracks, which included *Ultralight Beam, Father Stretch My Hands Pt. 1, Famous, Feedback*, and *Waves*. The recording, released February 14, 2016 (Valentine's Day), was delayed because, according to West, Chance the Rapper wanted the song *Waves* to be included on the album.

A collaborative effort was also undertaken by Chance the Rapper with the recording stars

Scan here to watch the moving tribute of the late boxer Muhammad Ali by Chance the Rapper with the song *I Was a Rock* at the 2016 ESPY Awards

Macklemore and Ryan Lewis. Their album, THIS UNRULY MESS I MADE, contained the song *Need to Know*, featuring Chance the Rapper. It was released February 26, 2016, and appears as the album's eighth track.

Along with legendary NBA center Kareem Abdul-Jabbar, Chance the Rapper paid tribute to the late boxer and "The Greatest" Muhammad Ali, who had recently passed away at his home in Louisville, Kentucky. The tribute, which took place at the 2016 ESPY Awards on July 13, 2016, featured a song that Chance the Rapper wrote specifically for the occasion, titled *I Was a Rock*.

The third day of Lollapalooza 2017 was headlined by Chance the Rapper in his hometown of Chicago. The event took place at Grant Park, located in the city's east downtown area not too far from the shores of Lake Michigan. He performed to record crowds; it was estimated that his performance drew some of the largest crowds in history of the event, which has been held off and on since 1991.

According to the site Ranker, the following are the top five collaboration efforts of Chance the Rapper with other artists:

Baby Blue by Action Bronson, featuring Chance the Rapper

(Released March 03, 2015)

This song is the last single off the second album of rapper Action Bronson, WELL-DONE. It represents one of the earliest collaboration efforts for Chance the Rapper, coming off the success of the release of his second mixtape, ACID RAP. *Baby Blue* sold half a million copies, earning a Gold certification from the Recording Industry Association of America (RIAA), and was featured during the 2015 YouTube Music Awards. The music video for this hip-hop song has over 23 million views on YouTube.

All My Friends by Snakehips, featuring Chance the Rapper and Tinashe
(Released October 25, 2015)

The British production duo of James Carter and Oliver Lee (Snakehips) released *All My Friends* as a single in October 2015. The song, an ode to youth and a series of bad nights while living in London, reached number five on the UK Official Singles Charts. A live performance of the song featuring Snakehips, Tinashe, and Chance the Rapper took place on February 25, 2016, on the *Jimmy Kimmel Live!* show on ABC television. The music video for this song has over 41 million views on YouTube.

Snakehips by Ross Brewer

Show Me Love (*Skrillex Remix*) by Hundred Waters, featuring Chance the Rapper, Moses

John Moore, aka Skrillex

Sumney, and Robin Hannibal
(Released March 22, 2016)

    Show Me Love was released as part of the discography of the group Hundred Waters. The 2016 remix was the work of Los Angeles–born Sonny John Moore, aka Skrillex, and features the artistry of Chance the Rapper, Moses Sumney, and Robin Hannibal. The music video for this EDB ("dubstep") remix song has over 20 million views on YouTube.

Penthouse Floor by John Legend, featuring Chance the Rapper
(Released November 18, 2016)

    Penthouse Floor is the second song from the DARKNESS AND LIGHT album of Grammy Award–winning artist John Legend. Chance the Rapper is featured in the song alongside Legend. The video shows Legend as a worker during a "Black Lives Matter" event, attempting to bring unity and strike common ground among diverse views in this country—a social commentary about the times we live in. The music video for this song has over 1.3 million views on YouTube.

I'm the One by DJ Khaled, featuring Chance the Rapper, Justin Bieber, Lil Wayne, and Quavo (Released April 28, 2017)

This is the second single from the 2017 (and tenth) album of DJ Khaled, titled GRATEFUL. The song features a host of today's popular and hip-hop stars, including Justin Bieber, Lil Wayne, and Chance the Rapper. *I'm the One* had a series of number one rankings, with appearances on the UK Official Singles Charts and U.S. *Billboard* Hot 100. It was also featured in the 2017 year-end recap video *YouTube Rewind*. The music video for the song has over 878 million views on YouTube.

Justin Bieber

Words to Understand

bureaucrat: a term used to describe a person, typically unelected, who works for the government.

hone, honing: sharpening or refining a set of skills necessary to achieve success or perform a specific task.

prevalent: something that is common, predominant, often seen.

respectively: something separately considered in order of listing; an example would be a sentence stating, "One and two are first and second, respectively."

trajectory: A path or a line that is followed; a trajectory typically refers to something that is upward or moving higher, presumably toward greater recognition or success.

Mr. Bennett's Beginning

Growing Up

Chance the Rapper was born on April 16, 1993, in the West Chatham section of Chicago, Illinois, under the birth name of Chancelor Jonathan Bennett. His parents, Ken-Williams Bennett and Lisa Bennett, were politically connected people who could be considered career **bureaucrats**. They held positions in the office of Mayor Harold Washington (Chicago's first African-American elected mayor) and the Illinois attorney general's office, **respectively**. Ken-Williams served also with then US Senator Barack Obama as a campaign aide and as deputy assistant in the White House during President Obama's first term. Later, he was a regional representative of the US Department of Labor.

Chance the Rapper has a younger brother, Taylor Bennett, who is also a hip-hop artist under his own name and has released albums under his label, Tay Bennett Entertainment. The brothers were heavily influenced by the stylings of other hip-hop artists such as Kanye West. Chance the Rapper had the opportunity to meet Kanye at the outdoor music festival Bonnaroo in Manchester, Tennessee, in 2014.

Through his parents' political connections, Chance the Rapper had the opportunity to meet Barack Obama as a youth, which had some influence on the course of his career **trajectory**. When a young Chancelor Jonathan Bennett voiced to the forty-fourth president of the United States his desire to become a hip-hop artist, Mr. Obama remarked (in a very adult way), "Word."

The young would-be artist was originally slated to go to Washington, DC, when Obama was elected president in 2008, as his father was slated to serve in the administration as a deputy assistant to the president. A change in plans saw Chance the Rapper instead enroll in Jones College Prep, where he spent his four high school years **honing** the skills that would make him the hip-hop star he is today.

Getting Educated

Reese White, one of Chance the Rapper's old friends—whom he has known since middle school in Chicago—said of their growing up, "We would always be getting into trouble for distracting the class."

White, along with Chance the Rapper and several other friends, were members of Save Money, a project started by the group to launch their careers as rappers.

Much of Chance the Rapper's time during high school was devoted to writing raps and performing, influenced in part by Kanye West, as well as Michael Jackson and other artists. His musical influences also extend to gospel, jazz, soul, and R&B. A ten-day suspension in his senior year served as inspiration for his first mixtape, titled 10 DAY, which was released online while he was a senior at Jones College Prep.

Fast Fact 1:

Chance the Rapper's Chance Meeting with a President—On the radio show *Sway in the Morning*, President Obama mentioned in a 2016 interview that he had known Chance the Rapper and his family for years, ever since his father served as state director for then Illinois state senator Barack Obama. President Obama first met Chance the Rapper when he was eight years old, or, as the former first lady put it, "We have known Chance and his family since he was a wee little baby rapper."

Expanding Family

In 2014, Chance the Rapper announced that he and his longtime girlfriend, Kirsten Corley, were expecting their first child in July 2015. The couple first began dating in 2013, just before the release of Chance the Rapper's first digital mixtape 10 DAY.

A daughter, Kensli Bennett, was born in Chicago on September 16, 2015. Chance the Rapper is very guarded about the details of

Kensli and her life, first introducing her to social media via Instagram on the last day of 2016.

The couple split in May 2016 and have a co-parenting arrangement in place. The custody agreement was reached in Cook County court on March 20, 2017, allowing both parents to share the responsibilities for two-year-old Kensli while maintaining separate residences.

The arrangement, reached civilly, lets the devoted father spend time with his daughter, going to basketball games and other kid-related events. He has taken Kensli to see his favorite professional basketball team, the Chicago Bulls, and she has met the former president and first lady of the United States.

Musical Progress

The Illinois rapper's career as a musician began in 2005. At twelve years old in the sixth grade, he was allowed access to a Chicago studio operated by a cousin. This let him experiment with beats, and he begin developing the sound that became the signature for his career. Kanye West's debut recording THE COLLEGE DROPOUT and the song *Through the Wire* served as a foundation to Chance the Rapper's introduction to hip-hop. This work, along with the recordings of legends such as Billie Holiday, R&B and

Kanye West

soul great Sam Cooke, and others, helped shape the young artist's musical stylings—influences that are **prevalent** in his music today.

He performed multiple times in the YOUmedia Lyricist Loft, an event co-sponsored by Colombia College Chicago and the Chicago Public Library System. The performances, at the Harold Washington Library, located in downtown Chicago, resulted in a second place award for songwriting. The award inspired the musician to continue pursuing his career through his final years at Jones College Prep.

It also gave Chance the Rapper an opportunity to meet another famous Chicago politician: former mayor Richard M. Daley.

Chance the Rapper's early career aspirations not only received the attention and praise of a future president of the United States, they were also cheered on and encouraged by an unlikely fan—former Chicago mayor Richard M. Daley of the powerful Daley political family.

Becoming a Star

The young musician stepped into the role of recording artist through both an unfortunate incident and the marvels of technology. While a senior in high school in 2011, he was caught smoking marijuana, an offense that resulted in a ten-day suspension from Jones College Prep. He used the time away from his studies to complete a fourteen-song mixtape named for the suspension, called 10 Day. He released it on April 03, 2012, on the widely available music-sharing websites DatPiff and SoundCloud.

Using available technology to get his music to enthusiasts has become a trademark of Chance the Rapper's career. He bypasses the major record labels and offers his music to fans on a direct basis.

His debut production, 10 Day, was referred to as a mixtape and was uploaded to the music website DatPiff for instant consumption and downloading. It immediately gained an audience and propelled the budding artist into the world of hip-hop artistry. Also available on the music-sharing website SoundCloud, the mixtape has been liked 174,000 times and shared over 25,000 times on that platform.

These are very strong numbers for a debut artist on a music-sharing website with little to no marketing, fanfare, or name recognition, plus a complete lack of major industry backing. The mixtape not only marked the beginning of Chance the Rapper's career, it showed him that he could, in fact, become an artist of note.

The critical success that started with the online release of 10 Day has put his career on an upward trajectory ever since. Chance the Rapper was able to turn a negative experience into a positive, life-changing moment. It just goes to show that good things can arise out of a bad situation.

The Social Experiment

In addition to his successful, award-winning solo career, Chance the Rapper is a member of the Chicago collective named Save Money. The group features his frequent collaborator Vic Mensa, with whom he has created several mixtape collaborations.

Additionally, Chance the Rapper has served as the lead performer for the band The Social Experiment. The group released its first album, Surf, on May 28, 2015.

The Social Experiment consists of artists who want to promote the free exchange of music through digital download services such as SoundCloud. Group members, along with Chance the Rapper, include artists Nate Fox and Donnie Trumpet. Chance the Rapper used The Social Experiment as a launch point for both ACID RAP and COLORING BOOK.

Text-Dependent Questions:

❶ What former US president met Chance the Rapper personally when the young star was a child?

❷ What former mayor of Chicago did Chance the Rapper's father work for early in his political career? What Illinois politician did Chance the Rapper's mother work for?

❸ What is the name of Chance the Rapper's younger sibling? What type of work is he engaged in as an adult?

Research Project:

Chance the Rapper grew up in a professional household, with both parents holding positions of influence, contrary to the notion that all hip-hop stars hail from broken homes, are involved in gangs or drugs, or have spent time in prison. Growing up in a seemingly affluent home, however, does not appear to affect the way fans view his music or his talents as a hip-hop artist. Do some research and name three other hip-hop artists, present or past, who grew up in a household where a parent (or both) was engaged in a professional career—such as law, medicine, politics, or business. Also name the parent and the type of career/job they held. As a hint, one of the names may be a hero of the young artist Chance the Rapper.

Words to Understand

avid: having an ardent desire or unbounded craving for something; a description of someone who is a loyal supporter, with keen interest and enthusiasm.

avowed: something that you are known to be or closely associated with; openly declared.

icon: a symbol that represents something, such as a team, a religious person, a location, or an idea.

née: a word used to indicate that the name shown is different from that given to the person when born, typically when a birth name differs from a married name.

stratosphere: literally, the region of the atmosphere above the troposphere and below the mesosphere; figuratively, something seen as being at the highest point (out of this world, phenomenal).

Chance the Rapper
HIP-HOP & R&B

Chapter 3

Finding New Worlds to Explore

Venturing Outside of Music

The 2013 release of Chance the Rapper's second mixtape, ACID RAP, took his career from earthbound to off the planet and into the **stratosphere**. The critically acclaimed and successful effort by the young rapper put him on the map and firmly launched him into stardom.

Since his debut in 2012, Chance the Rapper has set a new standard for artists, particularly for those who are independent and not associated with a major record label. Kanye West offered him an opportunity to become a part of his GOOD Music label in December 2016. Chance the Rapper declined the invitation, as his popularity was rising—due in part to the huge commercial

Chicago White Sox pitcher Jack McDowell

success of his third release, COLORING BOOK. He instead chose to remain an independent artist and retain the freedom of not being associated with a label.

He has also redefined fashion for hip-hop artists in what *Esquire* magazine termed an "almost uniform." His style is so hip, yet relaxed and acceptable, that he has become somewhat of an **icon** to his favorite hometown major league baseball team, the Chicago White Sox—a love he shares with fellow Chicagoan former president Barack Obama, an **avowed** White Sox fan.

Commercials and Endorsements

Chance the Rapper was featured in an ad spot for the website MySpace during their relaunch, which happened in June of 2013. The ad also featured performers Mac Miller, Pharrell Williams, and the artist Schoolboy Q.

He also had the opportunity to shoot an online video for the clothing brand Dockers. The commercial, promoting the clothier's spring line, allowed Chance the Rapper the opportunity to discuss his style, how much he enjoys the process of creating his music, and his life in Los Angeles.

Hip-hop magazine *XXL* revealed on May 05, 2014, that Chance the Rapper was among the performers included in its annual freshman class recognition issue. The other up-and-coming performers who were named included Isaiah Rashad, Ty Dolla $ign, Rich Homie Quan, Vic Mensa, August Alsina, Troy Ave, Kevin Gates, Lil Bibby, Jon Connor, Lil Durk, and Jarren Benton.

In August 16, 2016, Chance the Rapper performed in a Nike commercial, "Unlimited Together." Directed by Hiro Murai, it featured the song *We the People* written by the young rapper. He also remixed the jingle for Nestlé in a promotion of its Kit Kat candy bar—the famous *Give Me a Break* jingle—on October 04, 2016.

When H&M stores' new campaign, the much-anticipated Kenzo x H&M ad campaign, began in September 2016, Chance the Rapper was right there. He is seen in the commercial wearing a neon-green-and-black tiger-print jumpsuit and a pair of rubber rain boots with bright green soles. He appeared in the ad along with model Iman, Vietnamese rapper Suboi, Rosario Dawson, Japanese musician Ryuichi Sakamoto, Chloë Sevigny, and 16-year-old climate-change activist Xiuhtezcatl Martinez.

Rebellion as a Fashion Statement

A trademark of Chance the Rapper's look is his number 3 baseball cap. In an interview he did with *GQ* that appeared online on February 14, 2017, the young musician addressed the issue of his love of baseball caps and answered the question as to how the number 3 cap has become closely associated with him. The mystery is actually quite a simple one—it represents the mixtape number for his award-winning production COLORING BOOK.

Although there were earlier mixtape releases after ACID RAP but before COLORING BOOK, Chance the Rapper recognizes it as his third official release. Coming up with a cover logo, font, and style to match the tone of the release became extremely complicated, and he found the simple, stated number 3 was all he needed. End of story.

As for his love for baseball caps as an important fashion accessory, the Illinois native mentioned that he has worn them since being forbidden to do so while in high school. Capitalizing on his adult freedom to wear a baseball cap shows a bit of his defiant side, which is definitely reflected in his music.

Chance the Rapper has had the opportunity to design signature baseball caps for the Chicago White Sox major league baseball team. The artist teamed up with MLB cap maker New Era to design three styles. The team made them available in its team gift shop at U.S. Cellular Field (formerly known as White Sox Comiskey Park and called Guaranteed Rate Field in 2017). A preview of the designs was released via the Twitter account of the Chicago White Sox (@whitesox).

The caps went on sale just prior to the team's home opener on April 08, 2016. Coincidentally—or on purpose—Chance the Rapper was given the honor of throwing out the first pitch at the game against the Cleveland Indians.

The Small Screen Calls

Blueprint

Scan here to watch Chance the Rapper and Pat "The Manager" Corcoran discuss how their approach to the music industry is redefining the meaning of "musical independence"

This documentary-style program was created for the web-based network Crunchyroll by Blueprint Television. In episode twelve of the first season, fellow Chicagoans Chance the Rapper and Pat "The Manager" Corcoran were featured. The show aired on October 09, 2017, and discussed how the pair's unique approach to the launch of Chance the Rapper's 2016 acclaimed mixtape COLORING BOOK—through Apple Music—changed the landscape for independent artists and producers.

The *Ellen DeGeneres* Show

Chance the Rapper appeared on a season fourteen episode of *Ellen* on September 15, 2016, along with Lil Wayne and 2 Chainz as musical performers. The three artists performed the Grammy Award–winning song *No Problem* from the mixtape COLORING BOOK.

The Eric Andre Show

Season two viewers saw Chance the Rapper appear as a guest, along with former Spice Girls member Mel B, in a December 2013 airing. Comedian and actor Eric Andre hosts this parody of low-budget public-access talk shows along with his sidekick, Hannibal Buress.

Jimmy Kimmel Live!

R&B singer Tinashe and the British electronic duo Snakehips, featuring Oliver Lee and James Carter, joined Chance the Rapper in the limelight in this February 25, 2016, episode on ABC. The artists performed the song *All My Friends* together, a collaborative work they created in 2015. The song reached

Scan here to watch Chance the Rapper, along with Tinashe and Snakehips, perform their 2015 collaboration *All My Friends*

RIAA-certified Gold status for single sales of 500,000 or more. The fourteenth-season *Jimmy Kimmel Live!* performance was the first live rendition of the song by any of the collaborators.

The Late Show with Stephen Colbert

October 26, 2015

Chance the Rapper made his debut appearance on *The Late Show with Stephen Colbert* in *The Late Show's* first season with its new host. He performed as musical guest on October 26, 2015, singing *Angels* from Coloring Book on the show, along with his group The Social Experiment and the artist Saba.

Leading up to the appearance, Chance the Rapper was teasing his fans. During an interview on New York's Hot 97, he said that he was going to be debuting a collaborative song he created with Colbert.

 Me and Stephen Colbert have been working on a song together, and it's gonna be released very soon. [Colbert's] amazing. I can't get that deep into it, but he's amazing.

Stephen Colbert

The "song with Colbert" was an inside joke between Colbert and Chance the Rapper; there was no song that the two wrote together.

June 07, 2016

Chance the Rapper made his second appearance on *The Late Show with Stephen Colbert* in June 2016. The episode, number 154, also included electronic dance music (EDM) DJ Skrillex (**née** Sonny John Moore). The two hip-hop artists performed their collaboration single *Show Me Love*. Colbert joked during the episode that it was his remix bit on the show that made the song popular.

Colbert was referring to an earlier segment of the same episode. Skrillex and Chance the Rapper appeared with Colbert as he discussed a new cereal from General Mills and they created a remix. It was named *Tiny Toast*, and Chance the Rapper supplied the lyrics:

Scan here to watch Chance the Rapper along with EDM DJ Skrillex and host Stephen Colbert performing a remix joke for General Mills' *Tiny Toast* cereal

"Not a serial number / Not serial like a killer / Talkin' a complete breakfast, pure tummy filler."

September 25, 2017

In the third season, episode number ten, fans of *The Late Show with Stephen Colbert* saw Chance the Rapper appear again. Not only was he a guest performer this time, but he also expanded into the duties of a guest host with Colbert. Fresh off his Grammy Award win for the recording Coloring Book, Chance the Rapper sat down with Colbert to discuss his Grammy win. A secondary topic was the rumors of Chance the Rapper's possible political ambitions as mayor of Chicago.

Also appearing on the show was Emmy Award–winning actor Sterling K. Brown of the NBC hit series *This Is Us*.

Lyric Breakdown

In March 2017, Chance the Rapper's song *Same Drugs*, from Coloring Book, was analyzed and discussed by a random group of young listeners in this show produced by REACT TV.

The "reviewers" were mixed in their opinion of Chance the Rapper's work. The opinions were varied on the meaning of his songs, his use of lyrics, and the overall meaning of the song to them on a personal level.

RapFix Live

June 19, 2013

During season four, Chance the Rapper sat down for a discussion with MTV personality Sway in *RapFix Live*, a show produced for the MTV network. Artists J. Cole and Wacka Flocka Flame accompanied him in this episode. Chance the Rapper showed off his skills in some freestyle rap at the end of the program, alongside the other guests of the show.

October 30, 2013

Chance the Rapper returned to MTV's *RapFix Live* for more discussion about the hip-hop scene with host Sway and artist Stalley in season four's episode number thirty-four.

The Tonight Show Starring Jimmy Fallon

May 05, 2016

The first appearance of the young artist on *The Tonight Show Starring Jimmy Fallon* occurred with guests Robert Downey Jr. (*Captain America: Civil War*) and comedienne Amy Sedaris (*Unbreakable Kimmy Schmidt*). He performed during the season three, May 2016 episode, along with artists Jamila Woods and Byron Cage.

Robert Downey Jr at the Los Angeles premiere of Unknown at the Mann Village Theatre, Westwood.

October 03, 2016

In season four, Chance the Rapper, along with guests actress Emily Blunt and chef Mario Batali, made a return appearance on *The Tonight Show Starring Jimmy Fallon*. He performed the song *Blessings*

(*Reprise*) with Anthony Hamilton, Ty Dolla $ign, Raury, and D.R.A.M.

Chance the Rapper also had an opportunity to sit down with host Jimmy Fallon to discuss why he offers his music digitally, direct to his fans, instead of through a major label or distributor.

November 16, 2017

This season five episode was the third appearance on *The Tonight Show Starring Jimmy Fallon* for Chance the Rapper. This time, his fellow guest stars were the country music superstar couple Tim McGraw and Faith Hill. He sat down with the former *Saturday Night Live* alum Jimmy Fallon to discuss his upcoming hosting duties for the weekend show, as well as his philanthropic work in Chicago on behalf of Chicago Public Schools (more in Chapter 5).

Jimmy Fallon

Saturday Night Live

December 12, 2015

Chance the Rapper made his first ever appearance on the comedy sketch show *Saturday Night Live* in season forty-one with the host actor Chris Hemsworth. Billed as the musical guest, Chance the Rapper performed the songs *Somewhere in Paradise* (with Jeremih) and *Sunday Candy*.

December 17, 2016

Almost exactly a year later, he got another "chance" to appear for the second time, also as the musical guest. The host, actor Casey Affleck, introduced him. For the audience, both live and at home, Chance the Rapper performed the songs *Finish Line/Drown* with Noname Gypsy and *Same Drugs* with artist Francis and the Lights.

He also showed off some of his comedic skills while performing a parody of a Run-DMC song called *Christmas in Hollis* alongside *SNL (Saturday Night Live)* regular Kenan Thompson. Then he appeared in a skit as one of the Three Wise Men in a poorly put together Christmas play.

November 18, 2017

Another year later, episode six of the forty-third season gave Chance the Rapper the opportunity to display more of his comedic acting chops. Appearing as host for the first time, he made the most of the occasion to highlight his versatility as a performer—not just as a hip-hop artist.

In one of the best moments on the show, Chance the Rapper appeared in a music video—along with *SNL* regular Kenan Thompson and artist Chris Redd—for a throwback, Boyz II Men–inspired performance of *Come Back, Obama*. Playing off the Chicagoan's close relationship with the former president, the video featured a 1990s-style music video, with the trio delivering a heartfelt musical appeal for President Obama to return and continue to lead the country. The jokes and commentary were well received!

The View

Chance the Rapper appeared on the midday show *The View* as a guest on June 01, 2017. In the twentieth-season episode, he was interviewed by the panel of Jedediah Bila, Joy Behar, Whoopi Goldberg, Sara Haines, and Sunny Hostin. They discussed a wide range of subjects, including gun violence in his hometown of Chicago; his appeal despite being an unsigned, independent artist; and his musical influences.

Scan here to watch Chance the Rapper sing with comedian Kenan Thompson and performer Chris Redd in this *SNL* video with an appeal to the former president of the United States called *Come Back, Obama*

Wild 'N Out

This MTV show was in its ninth season when the program airing on June 29, 2017, featured Chance the Rapper engaged in a comedy battle with host Nick Cannon. Performer Saba was also a guest.

Text-Dependent Questions:

❶ What is the name of Chance the Rapper's sophomore (second) mixtape that received critical acclaim and recognition?

❷ How many appearances has Chance the Rapper made on the NBC comedy sketch show *Saturday Night Live*? How many times has he hosted *SNL*?

❸ What Chicago-area professional sports team is a favorite of Chance the Rapper? What professional game does the team play?

Research Project:

Chance the Rapper is a huge sports enthusiast and supporter of Chicago-based teams. This is not unusual for entertainers, as witnessed by the number of celebrities spotted during professional sports broadcasts, such as director Spike Lee, an **avid** New York Knicks (basketball) fan. Name at least five hip-hop artists (past or present) who are closely associated with a local professional sports team (i.e., basketball, baseball, football, etc.). Identify the artist, the team, the sport, and the extent of their involvement with the team.

As a bonus, find out (1) which artist has an ownership interest in a team, (2) which artist owns a professional sports management agency (name the artist and agency as well as several players represented and their sport), and (3) as an extra bonus, name the artist whose nickname came from a famous baseball player (and name the player).

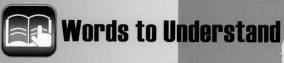

Words to Understand

accolades: awards or recognition that a person receives for their accomplishment or contribution to an effort.

genre: a subgroup or category within a classification, typically associated with works of art, such as music or literature.

innovation: the introduction of something new or different; a brand-new feature or upgrade to an existing idea, method, or item.

tireless: an effort that appears to never end, or continues without interruption or break; a tireless person is extremely dedicated to whatever he is doing and is willing to put forth tremendous effort and commitment to complete the task.

Chance the Rapper
HIP-HOP & R&B

Chapter 4

Chance the Rapper Builds a Name for Himself

Social Media Presence

Chance the Rapper distributes his music exclusively through digital platforms such as DatPiff and SoundCloud. This allows him to maintain his independence as an artist and frees him from any demands of being associated with a major record label. They would jump at the opportunity to sign the artist!

He promotes his appearances and comings and goings via social media accounts such as Facebook, and on Twitter (@ChanceUpdate), Instagram (@chancetherapper), and Snapchat (@mynamechance).

Streaming Availability

The Chicago native's music is available for streaming on each of the major music streaming and internet radio services. The list includes Spotify, iTunes, Apple Music, Pandora, and Google Music, as well as channels available on Last.fm, Slacker radio, and iHeartRadio. A simple search of the name "Chance the Rapper" will put you in touch with any one of the many tracks he has recorded so far in his short career.

The 2016 release of the mixtape Coloring Book was the first time he partnered with a major online music content distributor, and he chose Apple Radio. Apple Inc. paid Chance the Rapper half a million dollars for the right to be the first to distribute the production—which ultimately won a Grammy Award—digitally for two weeks in April, prior to its scheduled release on May 13, 2016. The exclusive deal with Apple Radio also gave Chance the Rapper the opportunity to market the work through Apple Radio with a 30-second spot presenting the song *Blessings (Reprise)*, featuring Ty Dolla $ign.

Awards Won

In his career so far, Chance the Rapper has been nominated for about twenty-five awards and has been the recipient of thirteen—only since 2016! These **accolades** and nominations come as recognition of his musical talent and contribution to the **genre** of hip-hop, which started in 2011.

Here is a listing of the awards Chance the Rapper has won during in his career.

BET Awards

Best Collaboration—*No Problem*,
featuring 2 Chainz and Lil Wayne | Won in 2017

Best New Artist Award—*No Problem*,
featuring 2 Chainz and Lil Wayne | Won in 2017

Humanitarian of the Year | Won in 2017

BET Hip-Hop Awards

Best New Hip-Hop Artist—*I'm the One*, featuring DJ Khaled, Justin Bieber, Quavo, and Lil Wayne | Won in 2016

Best Hip-Hop Mixtape Award—Coloring Book, featuring DJ Khaled, Justin Bieber, Quavo, and Lil Wayne | Won in 2016

Grammy Awards

Best New Artist—COLORING BOOK, featuring DJ Khaled, Justin Bieber, Quavo, and Lil Wayne | Won in 2017

Best Rap Performance—*No Problem*, featuring 2 Chainz and Lil Wayne | Won in 2017

Best Rap Album—COLORING BOOK, featuring 2 Chainz and Lil Wayne | Won in 2017

iHeartRadio Music Awards

Best New Hip-Hop Artist—*Ultralight Beam*, featuring Swizz Beatz, Kirk Franklin, The-Dream, Kanye West, and Cyhi the Prynce | Won in 2017

mtvU Woodie Awards

Best Video Woodie (Best Video of the Year)—*Everybody's Something*, featuring Saba | Won in 2014

NAACP Image Awards

Outstanding New Artist—*Life Round Here*, featuring James Blake | Won in 2017

Soul Train Music Awards

Best New Artist—COLORING BOOK, featuring James Blake | Won in 2016

Teen Choice Awards

Breakout Artist—*No Problem*, featuring 2 Chainz and Lil Wayne | Won in 2017

Speaking Out

Harvard University

Chance the Rapper gave a Q&A-style lecture at the Hiphop Archive & Research Institute at the Hutchins Center, located at Harvard University in Cambridge, Massachusetts, on April 20, 2015. The format allowed him the opportunity to field questions from students who attended on the relevant social issues of the day, including the Baltimore riots that happened that year, his work with Kanye West, and his use of streaming services. Some of the words he shared with attendees touched on the Baltimore situation:

> I think it's really most important for everybody to be informed, to be connected to the situation. I always say like there's an act—when to be a hand or to be a voice. You gotta know when your Twitter is stronger or your body actually marches. Sometimes it's either/or, you know? But I don't want to dance around saying this […] is wrong. I think we all know that. It's very hard to watch it happening on a loop.

And on the use of streaming services:

> Artist's space, you can upload your music whenever you want. You get the craziest metrics that anybody can offer you: sex, age, region of the world these people live in, a very detailed account of who's your fan and what they like.

2017 BET Award Acceptance Speech

It was a recognition-filled year in 2017 for Chance the Rapper. Not only did he win multiple nominations and accolades for his third release, COLORING BOOK, he also took home three Grammy Awards, three BET Awards, and two BET Hip-Hop Awards. One of the tributes he received was the 2017 BET Humanitarian of the Year Award, which honored his community work in Chicago. He provided $1 million out of his own pocket to help the financially struggling Chicago Public Schools.

The BET Humanitarian of the Year Award was established in 2002, and the award that first year was given to boxer and celebrity Muhammad Ali. It honors those African-Americans who have made significant contributions to their community, both in financial aid and in defense of other African-Americans. At only twenty-four years old, Chance the Rapper is the youngest person to receive the honor.

Not only was he surprised by the recognition, he received a special video introduction from Michelle Obama, a friend of the artist and his family. On the occasion of Chance the Rapper receiving the award, the former first lady said,

> *Barack and I are so sorry that we cannot be there with you tonight in person, but please know that we are with you in spirit, and we are so incredibly proud of you, Chance. We have known Chance and his family since he was a wee little baby rapper, and it has been a thrill watching him come into his own in so many ways. In addition to making some really amazing music, Chance has been taking that big bright spotlight that follows him around and he's shining it on young people in our hometown of Chicago. Time and again he has been standing up, speaking out, and doing the work to get kids in our community the education they deserve.*

Scan here to watch Michelle Obama's video introduction congratulating Chance the Rapper for receiving the 2017 BET Humanitarian of the Year Award and excerpts of his acceptance speech

Three Chicago Public School tenth graders penned an open letter posted on Billboard.com, thanking Chance the Rapper for his generous donation of $1 million. In their letter, the students mentioned their praise and appreciation and said, "There are many big celebrities from Chicago, but you are one of the few that really give back. It is evident that you sincerely care for the youth here. This is why you are an inspiration to us. We appreciate you for not only representing us through your music, but also through your actions."

Here is a transcript of the words Chance the Rapper himself shared as thanks while accepting the 2017 BET Humanitarian of the Year Award.

This is wildly overwhelming, I didn't think it was gonna be this crazy. I didn't prepare a speech, because I really wanted to see what would happen when I got up here and try and speak from the heart. . . .

I was gonna say, it feels a little early to get something like this, but my God doesn't make mistakes, and I like to think that he's putting this enormous pressure on me to see how I react. And I had plans originally to try and tell the world and everybody watching how to make it a better place. . . .

But my big homie [and childhood friend] Reese told me we gotta work on ourselves before we work can work on the world. So I wanna be a better father. I wanna be a better father to [my daughter] Kensli—I want to spend more time with her. . . . I'm a good man, and I'm gonna become a better man.

These are definitely powerful words for a young man so aware of how important it is to give back to the community!

Hard Work Pays Off

Chance the Rapper has worked hard and **tirelessly** for the success he has earned. Beginning with a ten-day suspension in high school and the release of his mixtape 10 Day, he has decided to overcome any difficulties and dedicate himself to becoming a successful hip-hop artist.

He thrives while inspiring his fellow artists and fans alike and creates a space where everyone feels empowered to pursue their own dreams. For him, dreams have been fulfilled by more than just "chance." The awards and accolades he has been nominated for are a small part of his achievements as an artist. The number of awards he's won is exciting in itself, but they are a just reward for all of the effort he puts forth as a recording artist. Chance the Rapper is certainly an evolving figure in the world of hip-hop. In a short period, he has become an artist to watch.

The blending of different genres—jazz, gospel, soul, R&B—has set his music apart.

His style is seen as a driving force in producing new content in the genre, and this level of **innovation** is key to attracting new audiences and keeping hip-hop relevant.

Chance the Rapper is frank about his struggles with religion, having been raised Christian with a strong influence from his grandmother, a woman he refers to as "Mama Jann." At one point, when it seemed that he was not going to reach his potential in life, Mama Jann prayed for him in a way that he described in an interview with *GQ* magazine as a "curse." Her strong influence and presence in his life, along with that of his parents, Ken-Williams and Lisa, shows that solid upbringing in his actions, and sometimes in gospel references in his songs.

Text-Dependent Questions:

❶ How many Grammy Awards has Chance the Rapper been nominated for? How many Grammy Awards has he won?

❷ Which organization honored Chance the Rapper with a Humanitarian of the Year Award in 2017?

❸ What genres of music have greatly influenced Chance the Rapper's style?

Research Project:

Chance the Rapper's recognition at the 2017 Grammy Awards, as an artist whose primary distribution outlet for his music has been digital, is certainly inspiring for any up-and-coming artist. Do some research online and identify other performers who have been as recognized as independent artists. By "independent artists," we mean those who have not received major backing from a large established record label such as Arista, Columbia, and Sony.

501(c)(3) charitable organization: an organization created under the Internal Revenue Code section 501(c)(3) for the purposes of engaging in social-, community-, and humanitarian-based charitable works on a nonprofit (no profit) basis.

disparity: a large, noticeable difference between groups.

enclave: a subdivision, or area within a larger established one, that may be either ethnically or culturally distinct.

eradication: the act of destroying or getting rid of something to the point that it is as if it never existed.

IRS: the Internal Revenue Service, a bureau of the US Department of Treasury, responsible for tax collection and the enforcement of tax policy in the United States.

Chapter 5

Supporting the Community and the Industry

Spearheading Education Changes

A growing issue that Chance the Rapper has brought much attention to is that of the education divide between inner-city school-aged children and those growing up in more affluent areas. Chance the Rapper grew up in the middle-class **enclave** of West Chatham in Chicago. Formerly an all-white neighborhood, African-American residents began settling in the area in the 1950s, resulting in a population shift from all-white residents to nearly all-black.

The area's affluence, and number of middle-class and college-educated individuals, made the neighborhood different from other African-American communities in the city, aside from the more affluent neighborhoods of Kenwood, Pill Hill, and Hyde Park (home to former president Barack and first lady Michelle Obama).

The West Chatham rapper benefitted from growing up in an environment that was more economically stable than those of other African- American students. His parents worked for influential people and had access to information and resources that allowed him to get into a highly competitive school like Jones College Prep.

The school, according to the *U.S. News & World Report* (noted for scoring high schools, colleges, and universities), ranks number three in the state of Illinois and number 110 overall in the United States—out of nearly 38,000 public and private high schools in the country. Of the students attending Jones College Prep in the 2015–2016 school year, 88 percent of them enrolled to take advanced placement (AP) testing, while 90 percent of those students passed an AP exam. That number is more than twice that of seniors graduating from Chicago Public Schools (40.6 percent as of the 2015–2016 school year).

The **disparity** between rich and poor students (and African-American and white students) has created significant educational achievement gaps. This prompted Chance the Rapper to begin the work of organizing a charity, SocialWorks, as an effort to provide needed funding to the otherwise underfunded Chicago Public Schools. He also uses the nonprofit organization to create spaces that will spur innovation and provide a constructive outlet for creativity—such as the one made available to him at Jones College Prep.

Fast Fact 4:

According to a study by the Urban League, an education gap of twenty-six points exists in the state of Illinois between African-American and white students. In the city of Chicago, this disparity is thirty-seven points. One of the factors leading to this gap is the difference in wealth between poor neighborhoods and rich ones. Property taxes are used primarily to determine funding for a school district, so the more affluent a neighborhood is (with stable and rising property values), the more property taxes are available to fund better schools. Since African-American students in Chicago tend to concentrate in low economic (poor) areas, they are more likely to be deprived of the same resources available to white students in higher economic areas of the city.

Chance the Rapper
HIP-HOP & R&B

Music Industry Support

In mid-2017, uncertainty over the future of SoundCloud—the digital download platform that Chance the Rapper uses, along with DatPiff.com—caused speculation that he would drop the service. A telephone call was reported between Chance the Rapper and SoundCloud's CEO Alex Ljung in July 2017. They discussed the service's future and the rumors of its demise. After receiving assurances from Ljung regarding the streaming platform's situation, Chance the Rapper sent out a tweet to fans dispelling any speculation that he was leaving SoundCloud. "SoundCloud is here to stay," was the message.

Along with colleague Young Thug, Chance the Rapper released an exclusive download titled *Big B's* as a show of support for SoundCloud on July 14, 2017. Within two days, it surpassed 1.3 million plays.

This type of industry support for a crucial platform for getting artists' music out to the public is an deed that Chance the Rapper did not hesitate to undertake.

Charitable Activities

Chance the Rapper has been involved in a few charitable and social awareness events in his career. This includes involvement in former president Obama's leadership summit in October and November of 2017; a special concert for the benefit of his charity SocialWorks—for his twenty-fourth birthday—on April 16, 2017; and his participation in the 88th Annual Bud Billiken Parade in Chicago on August 12, 2017, which is the largest African-American parade in the United States. In addition, Chance the Rapper's charity, SocialWorks, and its volunteers handed out 30,000 backpacks to Chicago-area schoolchildren.

Scan the code to watch Chance the Rapper discuss, on *The Tonight Show Starring Jimmy Fallon*, the reasons for starting the **501(c (3)** charity SocialWorks, and the fundraising and awareness-raising efforts of the organization

SocialWorks

SocialWorks is a **501(c)(3) charitable organization** created by Chance the Rapper and registered with the **IRS** in 2016. Its mission is "to empower youth through the arts, education, and civic engagement. SocialWorks will develop original programming and support the activities of other organizations that are consistent with their mission." The organization's mission, more simply stated, is "to inspire creativity, to build dreams, to let you, be you."

The efforts of SocialWorks have created partnerships with the Chicago Public Schools, Chicago Mayor Rahm Emanuel's office, and others (such as the car-sharing service Lyft) to provide much-needed resources to the schools and schoolchildren.

The organization has several program areas that are focused on helping students and inner-city youth break the cycle of poverty and become successful in life. These are in addition to supporting the Chicago Public Schools, an effort that has raised more than $2 million to date.

Kids of the Kingdom

This summer school program is available to Chicago youth. It provides educational opportunities to mostly disadvantaged children and a chance to travel to areas they may not otherwise see outside of their neighborhood. The children participate in interactive field trips and structured learning activities.

OpenMike

This venture is a monthly collaborative effort between SocialWorks and the Chicago Public Library. The events are held at the Cindy Pritzker Auditorium, which is located at the Central Library location in downtown Chicago. It's open to high school students as a space to share, teach, and inspire, and where they can practice and display their performative works in a supportive and encouraging environment. There have been twenty-five OpenMike events, with more than 3,000 minutes (51 hours) of performances and nearly 5,900 attendees.

The Harold Washington Library in downtown Chicago, IL

Parade to the Polls

This nonpartisan voter awareness and education project is designed to encourage first-time voters to register. It also empowers people at the polls through education and awareness.

Warmest Winter

In a partnership with the Detroit nonprofit The Empowerment Plan, this effort began in December 2015. The initiative provides warm coats to Chicago residents who are in need of protection during the harsh winter months, including those members of Chicago's "highly mobile community" (a term for homelessness). The effort has provided over 1,000 winter coats to persons in need.

Political Aspirations?

A website has been launched titled "ChanoforMayor"—a nickname for the rapper—that is encouraging the young artist, entrepreneur, and social activist to consider running for the office of mayor of Chicago in 2019.

There has been no word as to whether Chance the Rapper is interested in accepting a pay cut. The current yearly salary for the Chicago mayor is $216,210, which is far less than the hip-hop artist's 2016 income as reported by *Forbes*: $33 million.

He also hasn't mentioned if he truly has any governmental ambitions, but it should be noted that politics is in his blood and has been the family business for as long as he has been alive.

Conclusion

Winning the 2017 BET Humanitarian of the Year Award was a significant step forward in the career of Chance the Rapper. It showcased the fact that he has a good sense of his place in society, not only as a performer but also as a leader and as a philanthropist. If you listen to what people are saying about the artist, you hear praise and accolades for his work on behalf of youth to become better citizens, decrease the incidence of violence, and increase peace and understanding.

Maybe one day we will see Chancelor Jonathan Bennett—or rather, Chance the Rapper—sitting behind the mayor of Chicago's desk running the Windy City. Or maybe we'll see him someday sitting behind a bigger desk at 1600 Pennsylvania Avenue NW in Washington, DC!

Text-Dependent Questions:

❶ What is the name of Chance the Rapper's 501(c)(3) organization? What year was the charity first organized?

❷ What was the percentage students attending Chance the Rapper's former high school (William Jones College Preparatory High School) who received advanced placement (AP) testing? What was the AP pass rate of those students attending Jones College Prep, according to *U.S. News & World Report*?

❸ Which organization assisted Chance the Rapper's charity in providing over one thousand coats to people in need of sufficient outerwear?

Research Project:

Philanthropy and being a celebrity are things that should go hand-in-hand. There are many examples of entertainers from all areas—including film and television, sports, and music—who give plenty of their money to provide for those in need, or who donate funds when an emergency strikes. Chance the Rapper appears to be the type of celebrity that takes the mission of giving a step further, identifying a specific problem and advocating for its **eradication**. What other entertainers—specifically, hip-hop artists—raise money and advocate on behalf of a specific cause such as education, poverty, or community relations with the police? Identify the artist, the issue, and their efforts as an advocate—not only in contributing money but also offering public support through their actions. Identify at least three artists.

Series Glossary of Key Terms

A&R: an abbreviation that stands for Artists and Repertoire, which is a record company department responsible for the recruitment and development of talent; similar to a talent scout for sports.

ambient: a musical style that relies on electronic sounds, gentle music, and the lack of a regular beat to create a relaxed mood for the listener.

brand: a particular product or a characteristic that serves to identify a particular product; a brand name is one having a well-known and usually highly regarded or marketable word or phrase.

cameo: also called a cameo role; a minor part played by a prominent performer in a single scene of a motion picture or a television show.

choreography: the art of planning and arranging the movements, steps, and patterns of dancers.

collaboration: a product created by working with someone else; combining individual talents.

debut: a first public appearance on a stage, on television, or so on, or the beginning of a profession or career; the first appearance of something, like a new product.

deejay (DJ): a slang term for a person who spins vinyl records on a turntable; aka a disc jockey.

demo: a recording of a new song, or of one performed by an unknown singer or group, distributed to disc jockeys, recording companies, and the like, to demonstrate the merits of the song or performer.

dubbed: something that is named or given a new name or title; in movies, when the actors' voices have been replaced with those of different performers speaking another language; in music, transfer or copying of previously recorded audio material from one medium to another.

endorsement: money earned from a product recommendation, typically by a celebrity, athlete, or other public figure.

entrepreneur: a person who organizes and manages any enterprise, especially a business, usually with considerable initiative and at financial risk.

falsetto: a man singing in an unnaturally high voice, accomplished by creating a vibration at the very edge of the vocal chords.

genre: a subgroup or category within a classification, typically associated with works of art, such as music or literature.

hone, honing: sharpening or refining a set of skills necessary to achieve success or perform a specific task.

icon: a symbol that represents something, such as a team, a religious person, a location, or an idea.

innovation: the introduction of something new or different; a brand-new feature or upgrade to an existing idea, method, or item.

instrumental: serving as a crucial means, agent, or tool; of, relating to, or done with an instrument or tool.

jingle: a short verse, tune, or slogan used in advertising to make a product easily remembered.

mogul: someone considered to be very important, powerful, and in charge; a term usually associated with heads of businesses in the television, movie studio, or recording industries.

performing arts: skills that require public performance, as acting, singing, or dancing.

philanthropy: goodwill to fellow members of the human race; an active effort to promote human welfare.

public relations: the activity or job of providing information about a particular person or organization to the public so that people will regard that person or organization in a favorable way.

sampler: a digital or electronic musical instrument, related to a synthesizer, that uses samples, or sound recordings, of real instruments (trumpet, violin, piano, etc.) mixed with excerpts of recorded songs and other interesting sounds (sirens, ocean waves, construction noises, car horns, etc.) that are stored digitally and can be replayed by a triggering device, like a sequencer, electronic drums, or a MIDI keyboard.

single: a music recording having two or more tracks that is shorter than an album, EP, or LP; also, a song that is particularly popular, independent of other songs on the same album or by the same artist.

Further Reading

Bolo, Bern. *Chance the Rapper: Flying High to Success, Weird and Interesting Facts on Chancellor Jonathan Bennett!* CreateSpace Independent Publishing Platform, 2017.

Coval, Kevin, Lansana, Quraysh Ali, and Marshall, Nate. *The BreakBeat Poets: New American Poetry in the Age of Hip-Hop.* Haymarket Books, 2015.

Knight, Know Dan Edward Sr. *Who Is Chance the Rapper Who Supports Education: Is He a Modern-Day Savior for Kids? (Volume 1).* CreateSpace Independent Publishing Platform, 2017.

Meseke, Mitch. *The Illustrated Guide to Hip-Hop A–Z.* Independently published, 2017.

Ridenhour, Carlton Douglas ("Chuck D"). *This Day in Rap and Hip-Hop History.* Octopus, 2017.

Internet Resources

www.billboard.com
The official site of *Billboard Music*, with articles about artists, chart information, and more.

www.thefader.com/
Official website for a popular New York City–based music magazine.

www.hiphopweekly.com
A young adult hip-hop magazine.

www.thesource.com/
Website for a bimonthly magazine that covers hip-hop and pop culture.

www.vibe.com/
Music and entertainment website and a member of *Billboard Music*, a division of Billboard-Hollywood Reporter Media Group.

chanceraps.com/
Chance the Rapper's official website, which is the source for all news, updates, upcoming initiatives, and information about the artist.

Citations

"The Authority in Free Mixtapes" by DatPiff.com. http://www.datpiff.com. Accessed December 13, 2017.

"I found Chance the Rapper's old Facebook [account] yesterday..." by "Lavmar." MTV.com Staff "Chance The Rapper's Early Mixtapes Hit the Internet." MTV.com. December 11, 2013.

"Word" by President Barak Obama. James, Andy. "For Chance the Rapper & His Father, Things Come Full Circle." *DJ Booth*, Complex.com. October 19, 2016.

"We would always be getting into trouble..." by Reese White. Obaro, Tomi. "2015 CHICAGOANS OF THE YEAR: Chance the Rapper." *Chicago Magazine*. November 17, 2015.

"We have known Chance and his family..." by Michelle Obama. Williams, Alexis Paige. "The Video of Michelle Obama's Speech about Chance the Rapper at the 2017 BET Awards Will Make You Tear Up." Bustle.com. June 25, 2017.

"...almost uniform..." by Christine Flammia. Flammia, Christine. "Chance the Rapper Has Perfected the Almost-Uniform." *Esquire*. October 11, 2017.

"Me and Stephen Colbert have been working..." by Chance the Rapper in an interview with New York radio station Hot 97. Sharp, Elliott. "Stephen Colbert Made a Song with Chance the Rapper." RedBull.com. October 27, 2015.

"Not a serial number/ Not serial like a killer..." by Chance the Rapper. Holub, Christian. "Chance the Rapper and Skrillex Remix Stephen Colbert's Monologue." EW.com. June 08, 2016.

"There are many big celebrities from Chicago..." by Alex Rojas, Alondra Cerros, and Annelisse Betancourt, Lake View High School students. "An Open Letter to Chance the Rapper from Chicago Students: 'You're More Than Just an Artist to Us, You Are a Way of Life.'" Billboard.com. March 15, 2017.

"I think it's really most important for everybody to be informed..." by Chance the Rapper. Leight, Elias. "All The Best Quotes from Chance the Rapper's Lecture at Harvard." *The Fader*. May 06, 2015.

"Artist's space, you can upload your music whenever you want. You get the craziest metrics..." by Chance the Rapper. Leight, "All the Best Quotes..." 2015.

"Barack and I are so sorry..." by Michelle Obama. Williams, "The Video of Michelle Obama's Speech..." 2017.

"This is wildly overwhelming, I didn't think..." by Chance the Rapper. Spanos, Brittany. "Watch Chance the Rapper's Impassioned Call-to-Action at BET Awards." *Rolling Stone*. June 26, 2017.

"...Mama Jann..." by Chance the Rapper. Barnes, Tom. "Chance the Rapper's Life Story Told through 24 of His Best Lyrics." Mic.com. April 15, 2017.

"...curse..." by Chance the Rapper. Barnes, "Chance the Rapper's Life Story..." 2017.

"SoundCloud is here to stay," by Chance the Rapper. Carmichael, Rodney. "Chance the Rapper and Young Thug Dedicate 'Big B's' to SoundCloud." NPR Music News. July 17, 2017.

"...to empower youth through the arts, education and civic engagement..." by SocialWorks Chicago. "About." SocialWorksChi.org. http://www.socialworkschi.org/about. Accessed December 13, 2017.

"...highly mobile community..." by SocialWorks Chicago. "Warmest Winter Chicago: EMPWR Coat Initiative." SocialWorksChi.org. http://www.socialworkschi.org/warmestwinter. Accessed December 13, 2017.

Educational Video Links

Photo Credits

Index

Index

Index

Author's Biography

Joe L. Morgan is a father, author, and budding saxophonist. A music enthusiast all of his life, he shares his love of every type of music with his children, family, and friends, from modern jazz to dance and hip-hop.